summertime treats

summertime treats

recipes and crafts for the whole family

by sara perry

photographs by jonelle weaver

CHRONICLE BOOKS

SAN FRANCISCO

Library of Congress Cataloging-in-Publication Data:

Perry, Sara.
  Summertime treats / by Sara Perry.
    p.   cm.
  Includes index.
  ISBN 0-8118-2323-7 (pbk.)
  1. Cookery. 2. Handicraft. 3. Summer. I. Title.
  TX714.P462 1999   98-33815
  641.5'64—dc21   CIP

Printed in Hong Kong.

Craft design and development by Kathlyn Meskel
Prop styling by Christina Wressel
Craft styling by Maggie Hill
Food styling by Bettina Fisher
Design and illustrations by Carrie Leeb, Leeb & Sons
Book composition by Suzanne Scott

Distributed in Canada by Raincoast Books
8680 Cambie Street
Vancouver, British Columbia V6P 6M9

10 9 8 7 6 5 4 3 2 1

Chronicle Books
85 Second Street, San Francisco, California 94105

www.chroniclebooks.com

Notice: This book is intended as an educational and informational guide. With any craft project, check product labels to make sure that the materials you use are safe and nontoxic. Nontoxic is a description given to any substance that does not give off dangerous fumes, or contain harmful ingredients (such as chemicals or poisons) in amounts that could endanger a person's health.

The Art & Creative Material Institute in Boston certifies nontoxic supplies. Look for their seal of approval on art and craft product labels. For a complete product list of nontoxic brands (as well as those to avoid), write or call the institute at 100 Boylston Street, Suite 1050, Boston, MA 02116; Phone: 617-426-6400.

To Mom, Dad, and Mark,
To Pete, Matthew, Julie, and Dylan Paul,
To sweet summers past
and the happy summers to come

Over the years that I have been cooking, I have watched my mother, Martha Wheaton, create and prepare hundreds of delicious meals. She was the first to show me how rewarding it could be to prepare food for those you love. As a food writer and radio commentator, I have eaten marvelous food prepared by friends, colleagues, and perfect strangers. I have tested and tasted their recipes. I am thankful to every one of these valuable teachers.

I'm also indebted to those cooks I have never met but whose books and articles have helped me discover delicious ways to enjoy the summertime. Icy lemonade, sun-ripened tomato salad, and hand-shaken, homemade ice cream have refreshed people for centuries. They are not new to this book; they belong to everyone.

I thank all those generous people who have shared family recipes or ideas for summertime treats, especially Bette Sinclair, Fahti Rabizadeh, Barbara Morgan, Karen Brooks, Lena Lencek, and Bianca. A special thanks also goes to the staff of Friendly House, a Northwest Portland community center, for their useful ideas on how to keep summer kids happy.

This book has given me the welcome opportunity to work once again with Kathlyn Meskel. This time her attention is focused on crafts. She has an eye for seeing what works and a soul for knowing what gives pleasure. Her four-year-old son Jack has that same intuition. Thanks also to my friend Catherine Glass, who inspires tranquillity, serenity, and just the right words.

I am thankful to have a wonderful publisher, Chronicle Books, whose staff is as warm, friendly, and entertaining as a good summer reunion. Working with and knowing my editor Leslie Jonath is a gift. My thanks also to assistant editor Mikyla Bruder, who has the right tact and the good ideas, and to my editor Sharon Silva. And, as always, my gratitude, love, and loyalty to a real gentleman, senior editor Bill LeBlond.

table of contents

8 introduction

10 tips for cooking with kids

11 tips for crafting with kids

summer crafts and projects

14 pixie sand castles

15 how-your-garden-grows plant markers

16 one-for-the-road lunch box

19 sponge-painted patio pots

20 tiny terra-cotta lamps

22 fast and fun picture frames

25 ants-in-the-grass citronella candle

27 the big bug bucket

28 #1 dad gift tags and coupons

28 mother's heart's delight

29 cookie-cutter soaps

33 vacation place mat

summer thirst quenchers

36 sunshine tea

37 bianca's extra-lemony sidewalk lemonade

39 lime fizz

40 tropical cooler

41 banana smoothie

41 p-nut butter banana smoothie

42 mocha madness

44 piña colada shake

44 sweet strawberry lassi

45 pink flamingo punch

46 the ice cube

summer salads and snacks

50 dad's favorite deviled eggs

53 black bean and corn salsa salad

54 roasted greek potato salad

55 iceberg wedges with blue cheese dressing

56 tomato, mozzarella, and basil salad

57 orange mint tabbouleh

59 gazpacho-to-go

summer celebrations

62 *memorial day tailgate picnic menu*

62 super sub sandwich

64 *sunny sunday patio brunch menu*

64 melon–lemon sorbet compote

64 quick and simple centerpieces

67 sweet mama's morning cakes

68 *father's day barbecue menu*

68 grilled flank steak

69 *fourth of july barbecue menu*

69 fourth of july star-spangled celebration

70 a mixed summer grill

71 grilled corn on the cob
with flavored butters

73 clare's potato salad

75 fresh strawberry shortcake
with summer cream

77 stars and stripes dinnerware

80 checkerboard star picnic tablecloth

81 red, white, and blue parade wand

summer sweets

84 chocolate spanish peanut cookies

85 silver s'mores

86 blue-ribbon berry parfaits

87 fresh fruit cookie pie

89 neighborhood ice cream sundae

90 shake-rattle-and-roll ice cream

91 blueberry nests

93 five-spice peach blueberry crisp

95 chocolate p-nut butter candies

96 index

introduction

When I was six years old, my family began a summer tradition by spending Fourth of July at Malibu beach. While my brother, Mark, helped Dad load the station wagon with the Coleman stove, old blankets, and a canvas umbrella that smelled of seaweed and salt water, I was in the kitchen chopping egg yolks with a plastic knife for my dad's favorite deviled eggs. Mom let me stir in the Miracle Whip, lemon juice, and yellow mustard. I thought I'd done a magnificent job, but Mark wouldn't touch them. All the more for me, I thought.

The beach was hot and crowded. Blankets and people covered the sand, everyone hoping to get a view of the fireworks from the Santa Monica pier. We ate off the paper plates Mom and I had stamped with potato print stars, and it was just turning dark as we cleaned up. While everyone else was busy, I decided to share Mark's portion of my wonderful eggs. So, I slipped them out of the cooler and I went off in pursuit of a suitable family. When I found them, I decided to stay and try out the little girl's teddy bear sand mold. About the time the fireworks began, I realized my parents were nowhere to be found. Mom and Dad had made a similar discovery an hour earlier. After a police call and a frantic search, they found me. With tears in our eyes and egg on my face, I promised never to go off without telling someone first. It was the day I realized how much I loved my family.

Today, my family includes my husband, Pete; my son, Matthew; my daughter, Julie; and Julie's son, Dylan Paul, an adventurous cherub about to turn two. When my kids were growing up, they always wanted something to do. This book is for the kids who like to cook up a storm in the kitchen and like to do crafts, too.

Summertime is family time—whenever you get the time off from work. The food and crafts in *Summertime Treats* were developed with your family in mind. All are kid tested and approved. Your kids can handle most of the crafts and many of the recipes with minor assistance. Both the foods and the crafts are written in recipe form. The craft recipes list utensils you'll need in the list of ingredients to save last-minute tears and a frantic search for the disappearing stapler.

With the food recipes, you'll find suggestions for what your kids can do by themselves and where they'll need help. From counting fresh blueberries to squeezing lemons for lemonade, from making snakes out of no-bake peanut butter candy to measuring mayonnaise for a hot summer potato salad, there's something for everyone.

Food and drinks are divided into four chapters: Summer Thirst Quenchers, Summer Salads and Snacks, Summer Celebrations, and Summer Sweets. Summer Crafts and Projects start off the book. You'll also find some patriotic crafts in the Fourth of July section.

I've made two lists of helpful tips. One is for cooking with kids, and one is for crafts. Glance at Tips for Cooking with Kids when you're embarking on a great kitchen adventure. Check out Tips for Crafting with Kids when you're going to create something wonderful like the Pixie Sand Castles.

This book is about having fun, and I know you will. Leave room for kids of all ages to add their own creative touches, and they'll end up with special treats that are good to eat and great to use and display.

tips for cooking with kids

art box supplies

* Construction paper
* Crayons and colored pencils
* Decorative scissors, or pinking shears
* Drawing paper
* Felt pens and markers
* Glue sticks
* Paintbrushes, including $1/2$-inch flat-edged and $1/4$-inch round-tipped
* Paints—tempera, or watercolors
* Paper punch
* Pencils
* Resealable bags of shells and trinkets for decorating
* Ruler
* Scissors, round-nosed for safety
* Stickers
* Tape

* Review the recipe before you begin. (Ask an older child to read it out loud.) Be sure you have all the ingredients and utensils you'll need.

* Select a clear and clean kitchen counter, one with enough space to spread out all you'll need.

* Make sure everyone washes his or her hands with soap and water. A sneeze? A cough? A pat on the dog's head? It's time to wash those hands.

* Tie back long hair so it won't obscure vision or fall into the food.

* Store sharp knives and cooking tools in a safe place until they are needed. Wash knives, graters, and peelers separately. If they are all together in soapy water, someone might reach in and get cut.

* Have oven mitts handy to remove a hot dish from the oven or the microwave.

* Don't set pots on top of the stove with the handles sticking out. Kids—and even adults—can easily knock them over.

* Be sure children are careful around hot stoves or grills and that they know what to do in case of fire. If grease catches on fire, smother it with a lid, or baking soda. Never use water. Always have a working fire extinguisher in the kitchen, and make sure older children know how to use it. Double-check that every child knows how and when to dial 911.

* Use common sense and good judgment when you assign tasks to your young ones, and be close by to help with answers, difficult tasks, an extra hand, and lots of encouragement.

tips for crafting with kids

* Read through the Art Box and Around the House Supplies (this page and previous page), and stock up on the basics in advance. That way, you'll be ready whenever the mood strikes. Keeping supplies in a plastic storage container or shoe box will help make getting started easy.

* Select a work space. Craft projects can be messy, so choose a spot that's easy to clean up, well lit, and ventilated. Make sure there is a solid, flat surface on which to work that's big enough to accommodate the project you've selected.

* Line the work surface with waxed paper or a disposable plastic drop cloth. Have paper towels and a damp sponge on hand for quick cleanups.

* Read the project instructions all of the way through. Collect the materials you will need and arrange them on the worktable, ready to use.

* When it's time to get started, read the project directions to everyone who is participating. Or, ask an older child to read them out loud.

* Protect clothes with smocks, oversized T-shirts, or aprons. Better yet, turn an old set of play clothes into craft clothes.

* Lay out ground rules that will limit chaos and allow everyone to have a good time. Review safety precautions. Go over how craft supplies and tools are handled. Explain why some tools (hot-glue guns, knives, and aerosol sprays) need to be used by an adult.

around the house supplies

* Clear contact paper
* Clear plastic storage bags and twist ties
* Food coloring
* Masking tape and duct tape
* Paper towels
* Paraffin wax
* Saucers and small bowls
* Scratch paper
* Sharp paring knife
* Sponges
* Stapler
* Tweezers
* Waxed paper

Summertime is playtime. Long, endless days. Kids out of school. Good crafts and projects. Put them together and you'll have fun.

summer crafts and projects

Simple enough for the youngest artist, they leave plenty of room for the more extravagant expression of older hands. When time is short, it's a snap to stir up a batch of Cookie-Cutter Soaps, cure a case of the "I'm Bored Blues" with Sponge-Painted Patio Pots, and take your creativity on the road with Vacation Place Mats. All the instructions you need are right here.

pixie sand castles

Old 2-quart saucepan

2 cups sand (see note)

1 cup cornstarch

2 teaspoons cream of tartar

Wooden spoon

1½ cups hot water

Plastic wrap

Plastic drop cloth

Spoon, knife, and fork for
decorating

Small shells, paper flags, beads,
and trinkets for decorating

With a little sand and some help from the kitchen cabinet, you can build sand castles that no tide can destroy. A grown-up needs to be on hand to make the hard-to-stir sand mixture into pliable dough, but once that's done, kids can be turned loose to squish, pat, mold, and create their miniature marvels.

Makes approximately 4 cups sand dough, or two 4- to 6-inch castles

In the saucepan, combine the sand, cornstarch, and cream of tartar with a wooden spoon. Pour in the hot water and place over medium heat. Cook, stirring constantly, until the mixture is too thick to be stirred, 5 to 10 minutes. Remove from the heat.

Let cool until the mixture can be handled easily, about 10 minutes. Divide into 3 or 4 equal portions and roll each portion into a ball. Wrap each with plastic wrap and set aside.

Spread a plastic drop cloth over the work area. Unwrap each ball as needed to mold into a castle or other shapes, using the spoon, knife, and fork to form, smooth, and embellish the sand creation. Decorate with shells, flags, beads, and trinkets before the dough begins to dry. Repeat with the remaining balls.

Set the finished castles on a tray and allow them to harden for 2 or 3 days. Sprinkle any leftover dough with a few drops of water, wrap tightly in plastic wrap, and store in the refrigerator for up to 3 weeks.

Note: Bags of sand can be purchased at garden and home improvement stores, as well as some toy stores.

how-your-garden-grows plant markers

Create an instant garden gallery with your pixie Picasso's artwork as the main ingredient. With only a little help from you, vegetable rows and window boxes can be staked out in style.

Makes 7 plant stakes

Using the ruler and pencil, mark the card stock in $1\frac{1}{2}$-by-$8\frac{1}{2}$-inch strips. Give the card stock, crayons, and marking pens to your young artist. Older artists can draw a garden or pictures of the plants to be identified inside the lines. Let very young artists scribble first, and then you can mark the paper into strips.

After the artwork is done, using sharp scissors, cut the strips along the marked lines. With a marking pen, label each strip on the artwork side with the name of the plant to be identified. Add the date, name, and age of the artist on the back of each marker.

Measure and cut 14 pieces of contact paper, each 9 inches long and 2 inches wide. On a clean, flat surface, remove the backing from one strip, and place the strip, sticky side down, on top of one of the decorated strips. Smooth into place, making sure the surface is bubble free. Turn the decorated strip over and repeat. When both sides have been covered, trim the excess contact paper. Leave a thin, clear strip around each marker to keep moisture out. Cut the marker's bottom to a 2-inch point. Repeat the process with each strip.

keepsake bookmarks

Proceed as directed but instead of trimming the finished strip into a point, cut it straight across. You may want to use pinking shears for a decorative edge, or punch a hole at one end and add a ribbon.

Ruler

Pencil

$8\frac{1}{2}$-by-11-inch sheet white or cream card stock, construction paper, or plain manila file folder

Crayons

Marking pens

Scissors

12-by-18-inch sheet clear contact paper

Preserve mini masterpieces in the same way by adjusting the dimensions of the clear contact paper to fit the artwork.

one-for-the-road lunch box

A perfect send-off for any traveler, this lunch box doubles as a tour guide. Line the inside with a fold of waxed paper or foil, and it's ready to be packed with sandwiches, fruit, and snacks for hungry on-the-road appetites. The lid offers a handy look at the road ahead, with points of interest and welcome details.

Makes 1 travel lunch box

Cover a flat, clutter-free work area with 2 long sheets of waxed paper that overlap by 2 inches. Set the shoe box lid aside, and place the open box in the center of the work area, along with the paint and paintbrush. Brush only a light coat of the paint on the outside of the box so that it will dry quickly. When the first coat is almost dry, apply a second finish coat.

While the box is drying, lay out the map on a flat, clutter-free surface. Position the box lid over the map so that the travel route is centered on its top. Using the ruler and pencil, measure and mark a border all the way around the lid so that the map will cover the lid and fold over the edge of the shoe box lid with an extra 1/2 inch. Cut out the marked section of map, keeping the route of the trip centered on top. Wrap the lid of the box like a gift, folding the map over to the inside and securing it with tape all the way around the edge.

Next, mark the travel route with a brightly colored felt pen. Use small stars to mark fun side trips, clean rest stops, and your favorite points of interest along the way. Add postcard or brochure cutouts of the area and finish with stickers.

Waxed paper

Shoe box

1 bottle (2 ounces) craft paint, any color

Flat-edged paintbrush, 1 1/2 inches wide

Destination road map

Ruler

Pencil

Scissors

Tape

Fine-tip felt pens, in bright colors

Small star-shaped stickers

Postcards and brochures

Stickers with a travel theme

8 1/2-by-11-inch sheet white card stock

Glue stick

Measure and cut the card stock so that it will fit snugly inside the lid. Use more small stars and felt pens to list the starred points of interest marked on the map. Give brief descriptions and tips for travelers en route. Dot the back of the finished guide with spots of glue, and press it firmly into the inside of the lid.

variation

To make this box a permanent keepsake, add a light coat of gesso before painting. When the box is complete, brush on a coat of decoupage varnish to seal the box.

concert in the park?

Here's the perfect container for a picnic for two. Replace the road map with sheet music and the touring information with a concert program, musical facts, and trivia.

sponge-painted patio pots

In a single morning, your kids can make their own pretty patio flower pots or windowsill herb gardens by sponge-painting plain terra-cotta pots. The pots also make great containers for pencils and other craft supplies. Once you have mastered the basic technique, try cutting the sponges into simple shapes, and sponge-paint designs on your pots such as the ones pictured on page 18.

Makes 3 terra-cotta pots and matching bases

Cover a flat, clutter-free surface with long sheets of waxed paper so that they overlap by 2 inches. Have paper towels handy for cleanups. Pour 2 to 4 tablespoons of the selected craft paints into saucers.

Using a piece of sponge for each color, practice dipping and pressing the sponge on scratch paper to experiment with different effects. (Extra sponge pieces allow fresh ones to be used as needed.) Paint the first pot with the color selected for the first coat. Paint 1 to 2 inches inside the pot to create a finished edge. When the first coat has dried, use a new sponge and a contrasting color to add the top layer. Begin with a thin coat, using a blotting motion to cover the entire pot. Apply only as much paint as necessary to achieve the desired effect. A third color can be used if desired. Repeat the same process with each pot, as well as the pot bases. Add more paint to the saucer as necessary.

When the pots are thoroughly dry, place a stone or pottery shard over the hole in the bottom to provide good drainage and to keep the soil from dribbling out. If planting young plants, pour enough moist potting soil into your pot so that when you set the plant in the pot, the top of its root ball is about 1 inch below the rim. Continue filling in with soil around the root ball, tamping it down gently with your fingers.

Waxed paper

Paper towels

2 to 3 bottles (2 ounces each) waterproof craft paint, any complementary colors (see note)

Saucers for mixing and dipping paint

2 kitchen sponges, each cut into thirds

Scratch paper

3 terra-cotta pots, each 6 inches in diameter

3 terra-cotta pot bases, each 6 inches in diameter

3 stones or pottery shards

Potting soil

Potted plants (2 to 4 inches tall) or seeds for planting

Water

continued on next page

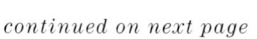

To plant seeds, fill the pot with soil and follow the seed packet directions. Water thoroughly.

Note: Painting directly onto terra-cotta gives a subtle tone to the colors. For a matte finish, paint the pots with a coat of gesso before sponging on color. To use the same color in lighter and darker shades, pour the selected color into two saucers, and lighten one with a few drops of white paint. For a glossy finish, cover with a clear acrylic spray after the paint dries fully.

tiny terra-cotta lamps

Your kids can help light the way to your next summer party with these tiny pots of light. They'll need 2-inch terra-cotta pots and standard ⅝-inch tea light candles, both found at a one-stop shopping center.

Little hands can arrange the pots on a baking sheet before they are put into a 200°F oven to warm for 15 to 20 minutes. Then they can pop the candles from their metal cases while bigger kids press them into the warmed pots. When the pots have cooled, make a game of tucking the lamps along walkways, garden steps, or on porch rails. The lights are magical.

fast and fun picture frames

Wooden frame (see note)

Decorating supplies, such as shells, small toys, pennies, and/or buttons

Rubber cement or hot glue gun

Clear acrylic spray (optional; see note)

This easy project offers quick, satisfying success. The amazing results make the frames perfect for gifts or for the family mantle. Kids will love to find and arrange the decorations for their picture frames. Adults should handle the glue gun.

Makes 1 frame

Remove the glass and matte from the frame and set aside in a safe place. Center the face of the frame on a clean, clutter-free surface, and gather the decorating supplies. Little helpers will have fun arranging and rearranging the different decorations on the frame until they are "just right." When a final arrangement has been chosen, a grown-up should glue the pieces into place. Allow the glue to dry following the product directions. If desired, spray on a coat of clear acrylic to give a glossy finish. Reassemble the frame.

Note: For easy decorating and gluing, select natural wood or solid-color frames with a flat, 1- to 2-inch surface. Avoid grooved or rounded frames.

Aerosol sprays should be handled with care by an adult. Follow the product instructions, and always work outdoors or in a well-ventilated area.

let's-play-jacks frame

Follow the above directions to take apart the frame. Paint the frame and one or several sets of jacks, including the ball(s), with silver, bronze, or gold metallic spray. Let dry well. Apply a second coat if you need better coverage. When the paint is dry, little helpers can arrange the pieces and a grown-up can glue them in place. If desired, spray with a coat of clear acrylic spray to give a glossy finish.

ants-in-the-grass citronella candle

This indoor project adds a fun twist to a patio essential. Citronella candles are commonly used outdoors because they contain a natural insect repellent. Working with warm paraffin and a hot glue gun takes an adult hand, but your kids can collect the grass, and trust me, they'll love deciding just exactly where the ants will crawl.

Makes 1 decorated candle

Place the candle, blades of grass, and plastic ants on a work area. Have paper towels handy for wiping up bits of wax.

Melt the paraffin in the top of the double boiler over boiling water.

With the tweezers, grasp a grass blade by its widest end and dip it into the melted wax. Hold the grass over the pan for a moment to allow the excess wax to drip free. Immediately lay the grass on the candle with the wide end at the base and the tip pointing toward the wick. Repeat all the way around the candle, overlapping shorter blades on top of the other blades to make the grass look as if it's growing. If the grass doesn't adhere, carefully wipe the spot clean with a paper towel and add a new piece.

Once the grass is in place, add the ants. Using the tweezers, grasp an ant, place a dot of hot glue on its underside, and attach it to the candle. Position the ants throughout the grass.

Caution: Paraffin will ignite if overheated or exposed to open flame. Always melt over water, preferably in a double boiler.

Note: Plastic ants can be found in craft shops and toy stores. Each package contains about 100 ants, and costs under $2.

Citronella pillar candle,
  8 inches tall

30 to 50 blades of grass, each
  3 to 6 inches long

Small black plastic ants
  (see note)

Paper towels

3 cups water

1- to 2-quart double boiler

1 cake paraffin wax (2 ounces)

Tweezers

Hot glue gun (see note, page 27)

the big bug bucket

This project was created by four-year-old Jack Meskel, who always knows exactly what he wants. He helped paint the pot, and told his mom where to glue the bugs. For a super easy bug bucket, purchase bug stickers and let your little one decorate a bucket like the one on page 26.

Makes 1 big bucket

Cover a flat, clutter-free surface with long sheets of waxed paper so that they overlap by 2 inches.

Working on the protected surface, brush a generous coat of gesso on the outside of the dairy container, using a thicker layer to cover lettering or logos. Wash and dry the brush. Have a roll of paper towels handy for cleanups. When the gesso is dry, paint the container with a coat of acrylic paint, then let it dry thoroughly. If necessary, apply a second coat.

When the paint is dry, let your kids select the bugs and decide where they should go, while you glue the bugs in place with the glue gun. To make a handle, use a paper punch to punch two holes in the bucket, directly across from each other and both about ½ inch below the rim. Make a knot at the end of a rope. Thread the unknotted end from the inside to the outside of one hole. Loop the rope over the top of the container, and back through the opposite hole from the outside to the inside. Knot it to secure the handle.

Notes: Jack's bucket was made from a large sour cream container. Large cottage cheese and yogurt containers also work.

A hot glue gun is recommended because the glue bonds firmly and dries quickly. Glue guns should always be used with care and only by adults.

Waxed paper

Flat-edged paintbrush, 1 inch wide

1 bottle (8 ounces) gesso

1-quart plastic dairy container with lid (see note)

Paper towels

1 bottle (2 ounces) acrylic paint, any color

20 to 30 plastic bugs

Hot glue gun (see note)

Paper punch (optional)

8-inch-length rope, ¼ inch thick (optional)

#1 dad gift tags and coupons

With a little help, even the youngest child can give Dad a special gift. Using construction paper, cut the shape of the number one and have the child decorate it with markers, crayons, and stickers. Then, using a marker, write on it "Good for 1 Giant Hug." Older kids can add their own ideas, such as "Good for 1 Free Car Wash," "Good for 1 Free Shoe Shine," or "Good for 1 Fishing Pal."

mother's heart's delight

A preschool artist can show mom how much she is loved with a handful of handmade hearts. Using construction paper in mom's favorite colors, cut out hearts and then call in the artist to decorate with markers, crayons, and stickers. Using a marker, write a promise on each heart. Mom will treasure the artwork as much as the coupon offers for "A Long Hot Bath," "One Day to Sleep In," or "We'll Make Dinner," especially when they are made in the artist's own hand, however squiggly and unsure.

cookie-cutter soaps

Quick and easy, cookie-cutter soaps are fun to make and use. Mom or Dad should be on hand to supervise, but even a four-year-old can create soap shapes with success, leaving only suds to clean up.

Makes 6 to 8 soaps, depending on size

Pour the powdered detergent into the large bowl. Add the water, ¼ cup at a time, stirring with a wooden spoon until it forms a thick batter the consistency of sticky play dough. Divide the mixture among the 3 small bowls. Add 2 or 3 drops red food coloring to the first bowl. (For a darker color, add more drops.) Coat children's hands with vegetable oil. Let them work the color into the dough until it is completely blended. Have them wash their hands and apply more vegetable oil before mixing a new color. Repeat with the green and blue food colorings.

Cover a flat, clutter-free surface with long sheets of waxed paper that overlap by 2 inches. Pour several teaspoons of vegetable oil into a saucer for dipping the cookie cutters. Have paper towels handy for cleanups.

With clean, oiled hands, pat out each portion of soap dough 1 inch thick. Dip a cookie cutter into the oil and, pressing firmly, cut through the soap. Carefully remove the cookie cutter. (If the soap shape sticks to the cutter, gently remove it with your fingertips.) With a spatula, place the finished shapes on a baking sheet lined with waxed paper. Set the sheet in a safe, dry place to cure for 24 hours.

Notes: If Ivory Snow is unavailable, use another gentle-care powdered detergent such as Dreft. Do not substitute heavy-duty stain-removal detergents that contain skin or eye irritants.

4 cups Ivory Snow powdered detergent (see note)

Large bowl

½ cup water

Wooden spoon

3 small bowls

Red, green, and blue food colorings

Vegetable oil (see note)

Waxed paper

Saucer

Cookie cutters

Paper towels

Spatula

Baking sheet, lined with waxed paper

continued on next page

Much in the same way a powdering of flour is needed for working with pastry dough, a generous coat of vegetable oil on hands (and even on the waxed paper or work surface) will make the soap dough manageable and easy to work. Otherwise it can be too sticky to handle. Keep an extra cup of powdered detergent on hand to add if the mixture is too sticky.

sweet hearts and flowers

Follow the basic recipe, adding 18 to 30 drops of essential oil such as lavender, rose, or vanilla. Divide the dough among 4 small bowls, and add 2 or 3 drops food coloring to each, making 4 different pastel shades. Continue as directed, using heart- and flower-shaped cookie cutters. Arrange the finished soaps in a small basket on a bed of tissue paper.

"you're the star" soap-on-a-rope

Proceed as directed, but leave the mixture in the large bowl. Omit the food coloring. Add 1/4 cup old-fashioned rolled oats or cornmeal and a few drops of an essential oil such as lemongrass, eucalyptus, or rosemary. With clean, oiled hands, roll the soap into a ball before molding it into the shape of a 1-inch-thick star. Using a straw or pencil, pierce one of the star's points at its base, piercing it all the way through. Thread a 2-foot length of 1/4-inch rope or twine through the hole. Tie the ends in a tight double knot and pull it back through to the center of the hole created for the rope.

vacation place mat

On a day trip or family vacation, collect postcards, brochures, maps, and any memorabilia with a flat surface. Put them together with photos, paper cutouts, and stickers to make a fun and festive collage.

Makes 1 place mat

Lay the construction paper on a flat, clean surface. Spread out the pieces you want to use in the collage so they can be easily seen. Little hands will enjoy cutting or tearing larger pieces into fun shapes and sizes. Arrange the pieces on the construction paper, leaving a $1/2$-inch border on all 4 sides. Tack them down lightly with spots of glue. Add stickers, cutouts, and finishing touches.

Position the place mat on a clean, clutter-free surface. Peel off the backing from a sheet of the contact paper. Carefully place the sheet, sticky side down, onto the collage, and gently smooth it into place. Working from one side to the other, smooth out any ripples or air pockets. Turn the collage over and repeat the process on the other side, sealing both sides together. Trim off the excess contact paper, using regular scissors or pinking shears for a decorative edge.

Note: Large sheets of construction paper are generally 12 by 18 inches, so 1 inch will need to be trimmed from both the length and the width. This will insure a moistureproof seal.

vacation scrapbook

Many three-ring binders have clear plastic covers into which you can slip a sheet of paper. Simply cut the collage slightly smaller than the cover and insert it under the clear plastic cover. Fill the binder with photograph sleeves and plain paper to make a scrapbook.

11-by-17-inch sheet construction paper, any color (see note)

Postcards, maps, photographs, leaves, or other flat souvenirs

Scissors

Glue stick

Stickers and decorative cutouts (optional)

2 sheets clear contact paper, each 12 by 18 inches

The best part of summer and sizzling temperatures is quenching your thirst with an ice-cold drink. In this chapter you'll find easy-to-make, cool family delights like misty fruit fizzes, tropical punches, and icy-silk smoothies. You'll

summer thirst quenchers

discover ways to have fun with your kids concocting frosty, fruity, and flavored ice cubes to chill and change simple juices, iced teas, and sparkling waters into extra-special beverages. Here are drinks your kids can whip up with a spoon or a blender and grown-up versions you'll want to stir with a swizzle stick under a rising moon. Every drink you make will be a refreshing surprise, like that first dive into a pool or a leap through the backyard sprinklers. Summer doesn't get much better than this.

sunshine tea

9 to 12 black tea or herbal
   tea bags

4 cups (1 quart) water

3 tablespoons sugar (optional)

1 fresh mint sprig, 6 inches long

Ice cubes, plain or flavored
   (page 46)

Here's a fun recipe for kids to make. Watching the water slowly turn the color of the tea is a little like magic. With all the various caffeine-free herbal and other teas available, you can make sun teas that all ages can enjoy.

Serves 4

In a large, clear plastic container with a lid, combine the tea bags, water, sugar, and mint sprig. Tighten the lid and shake gently. Place the jar in a warm, sunny place for 3 hours. During the first hour, the kids can check the jar every 15 minutes to see how the liquid changes color.

Remove the tea bags, squeezing gently, and discard. Remove and discard the mint sprig. Chill the tea.

To serve, pour the tea into a large pitcher. Fill 4 large glasses with ice cubes. Pour in the tea and serve.

bianca's extra-lemony sidewalk lemonade

Bianca is my eleven-year-old friend who knows nothing beats fresh lemonade on a hot summer's day. This recipe is her mother's, but Lena Lencek lets her daughter make it with just a little supervision while cooking the stove-top sugar syrup. For fifteen cents a glass, Bianca treats thirsty neighbors to her marvelous lemonade and her sunny disposition.

1 cup sugar syrup, divided (recipe follows)

12 large lemons, divided

6 cups water, divided

Serves 6

Make the sugar syrup. Divide the 12 lemons into two stacks of 6 lemons each. Using a citrus juicer, squeeze the juice from 6 lemons into the pitcher; you should have 1$^{1}/_2$ cups. Add $^1/_2$ cup sugar syrup and 3 cups water. Stir the lemon mixture and pour into ice cube trays. Place in the freezer until frozen.

Repeat the same recipe, using the remaining 6 lemons, $^1/_2$ cup sugar syrup, and 3 cups water. Stir the mixture, taste, and adjust the amount of water and sugar syrup to your liking. Fill 6 tall glasses with the frozen lemon ice cubes. Divide the lemonade among the glasses and enjoy.

sugar syrup

In a saucepan, over medium heat combine 2 cups sugar and 2 cups water. Bring to a boil, stirring until the sugar dissolves. Simmer for 10 minutes. Remove from the heat and let cool before using. Keep any unused syrup refrigerated in a covered container; it will keep indefinitely. Use for all those summertime pleasures when you want something cool and sweet to drink. Makes 2$^{1}/_2$ cups.

lime fizz

Every August, our family and our neighbors on either side get together for a Sunday barbecue. It's always the same menu: baby back ribs, spicy Italian sausages, and hamburgers for the kids. My contribution is easy: a tray with all the fixings for Lime Fizzes. Since the kids make lemon-lime sodas, I add lemon syrup to the tray so that they can mix their own. The Lime Fizz stands in as a mixer, too, for grown-ups who like their tonic with a touch of gin.

Serves 1

In a tall glass, combine the lime juice and syrup, then pour in sparkling water almost to fill, leaving room for ice cubes. Stir well, taste, and adjust the lime juice/lime syrup balance. Add ice cubes and garnish with the lime slice.

lime syrup

Scrub 4 limes under running cold water and pat dry. (At this point, you can squeeze the limes and reserve the juice, fresh or frozen, for other uses.) Using a zester, remove the zest. In a small saucepan over medium heat, combine 2 cups sugar and 2 cups water. Bring to a boil, stirring until the sugar dissolves. Stir in the zest and simmer for 10 minutes. Remove from the heat and let cool before using. Refrigerate any unused syrup in a covered container; it will keep indefinitely. Use to sweeten summer drinks. Makes 2½ cups. To make **lemon syrup**, substitute 4 lemons for the limes and proceed as directed.

adult fizz

Add gin to taste.

2 tablespoons fresh lime juice

2 tablespoons lime syrup (recipe follows)

Chilled sparkling water, club soda, or tonic

Ice cubes

1 lime slice

tropical cooler

½ cup pineapple chunks

½ cup papaya chunks

2 tablespoons coconut syrup (see note)

½ cup vanilla ice cream or frozen vanilla yogurt

¼ cup milk

½ cup small or coarsely cracked ice cubes

Imagine vacationing in Hawaii and spending part of each day at a white sand cove on Makaiwa Bay. Above the beach on a grassy knoll stands the Mauna Lani Beach Club, and inside the club is JoAnn, who makes the best tropical coolers I've ever tasted. She mixes fruits and syrups and vanilla ice cream in all kinds of delicious ways. For the adults, she adds platinum rum. Here's my rendition of one of JoAnn's drinks.

Serves 2

In a blender, combine the pineapple, papaya, coconut syrup, ice cream, milk, and ice. Mix at high speed until smooth. Pour into 2 tall, frosty glasses.

Note: Coconut syrup is available at most supermarkets in the coffee, tea, or condiment section. One popular brand is Torani. If the syrup is unavailable, or if you do not like the taste of coconut, substitute pineapple or orange juice or any other favorite fruit juice.

adult version

For grown-up tastes, there is nothing better than a **sunburn smoothie**. Simply add 1 jigger (3 tablespoons) light rum before blending the other ingredients.

banana smoothie

When my kids were young, they voted me "Number 1 Mom" at a family reunion because I let them have shakes for breakfast. See what fresh juices or fruits are available at the grocery store or farmers market and have fun experimenting with different flavors.

Serves 2

In a blender, combine the banana, orange juice, pineapple juice, yogurt, sugar, protein powder, and ice. Mix at high speed until smooth. Pour into 2 tall, frosty glasses.

blender blues?

If crushing ice cubes is a problem for your blender, eliminate the ice cubes, and freeze the fruit and yogurt.

1 small ripe banana, cut into chunks

$\frac{1}{2}$ cup fresh orange juice

$\frac{1}{2}$ cup canned unsweetened pineapple juice

$\frac{1}{2}$ cup plain yogurt

1 tablespoon sugar or honey to taste

Protein powder to taste (optional)

$\frac{1}{2}$ cup small or coarsely crushed ice cubes (see note)

p-nut butter banana smoothie

This yummy drink was concocted when my eight-year-old son, Matthew, was in a hurry to go somewhere. All he could find to mix in with the yogurt was a very ripe banana and some peanut butter. Chocolate lovers, substitute frozen chocolate yogurt, ice cream, or sorbet for the plain yogurt.

Serves 1

In a blender, combine the banana, peanut butter, yogurt, sugar, and ice. Mix at high speed until smooth. Pour into a tall, frosty glass.

1 small or $\frac{1}{2}$ large ripe banana, cut into chunks

1 tablespoon creamy-style peanut butter

$\frac{1}{2}$ cup plain or vanilla yogurt

2 to 3 teaspoons sugar or honey

$\frac{1}{2}$ cup small coarsely crushed ice cubes

mocha madness

2 cups small or coarsely crushed ice cubes

½ cup brewed espresso or triple-strength coffee, at room temperature

3 to 4 tablespoons chocolate syrup

2 teaspoons sugar

1 cup whole milk

Kids aren't the only people who need a sweet, slushy drink to keep them happy on a hot afternoon. This caffeine-loaded cooler will get your grown-up juices flowing for a softball game or that lawn-mowing chore you keep putting off.

Serves 4

Put the ice in a blender. Add the espresso, chocolate syrup, sugar, and milk. Blend until slushy. If the drink is too thick, add a little more milk and blend again. Pour into 4 frosty glasses, dividing evenly. Serve at once.

cola variation

For those who love cola, add ½ cup carbonated cola to the blender along with the other ingredients, and blend until frothy. Serve as directed.

adult versions

Add 1 jigger (3 tablespoons) each creme de cacao and coffee-flavored liqueur along with the other ingredients. Or add ¼ cup light rum.

piña colada shake

½ cup pineapple chunks

2 tablespoons pineapple juice

2 tablespoons lime juice

½ cup vanilla ice cream or
frozen yogurt

¼ cup milk

2 tablespoons coconut syrup
(see note, page 40)

½ cup small or coarsely crushed
ice cubes

*Rich and refreshing, this is a scrumptious shake for a party. When
Matthew and Julie make this drink for breakfast, they use orange juice
and frozen vanilla yogurt instead of lime juice and ice cream.*

Serves 2

In a blender, combine the pineapple chunks, pineapple juice, lime
juice, ice cream, milk, coconut syrup, and ice. Mix at high speed until
smooth. Pour into 2 tall, frosty glasses.

classic piña colada

Omit the ice cream and milk and add 2 to 3 tablespoons light rum.

sweet strawberry lassi

½ cup fresh or frozen hulled
strawberries

½ cup plain yogurt

1 teaspoon rose water (see note)

¼ cup milk or water

1 tablespoon honey or more
to taste

½ cup small or coarsely cracked
ice cubes

*A lassi is a chilled yogurt drink that is sometimes lightly perfumed
with rose water. When you add fresh strawberries, this healthy drink
takes on the taste of a summer garden.*

Serves 2

In a blender, combine the strawberries, yogurt, rose water, milk,
honey, and ice cubes. Mix at high speed until smooth. Pour into
2 frosty glasses.

Note: Rose water is stocked in the condiment section of most supermarkets. It is also available where liquor is sold.

pink flamingo punch

Everyone in your family will like this recipe because it makes so many different beverages. If you blend the fruit with frozen strawberries, you'll have a satisfying slush the kids will love. Add the soda and you've made Pink Flamingo Punch. Use vodka and triple sec in place of the soda and you've created Firefly Martinis for a cocktail party.

Serves 4

In a blender, combine the strawberries, watermelon, orange juice, lime juice, and sugar syrup. Mix at high speed until pureed. Strain through a fine-mesh sieve (or 2 medium-mesh sieves placed at right angles) into a pitcher; discard the solids. Add club soda and stir well.

Fill long-stemmed glasses with ice cubes and pour in the punch.

firefly martini

Place the strained juice in a martini pitcher or cocktail shaker. Omit the club soda and add $2/3$ cup vodka and $1/3$ cup triple sec. Fill with cracked ice. Stir with a long bar spoon or shake for $1\frac{1}{2}$ to 2 minutes. Pour into 4 cocktail glasses, taking care to strain the ice. Serve at once.

1 cup fresh or frozen hulled strawberries

1 cup seeded, diced watermelon

$\frac{1}{2}$ cup fresh orange juice

1 tablespoon lime juice

1 tablespoon sugar syrup, or to taste

1 cup club soda, chilled

Ice cubes

the ice cube

* For clear ice cubes, use bottled spring water or tap water that's been boiled and cooled to room temperature.

* Use good-tasting water to make ice cubes. If your water tastes bad, your ice cubes will taste worse.

* When using ice cubes for slushes, smoothies, and other blended drinks, make sure they are small enough that they can be evenly crushed in your blender. Small commercial ice cubes with hollow centers work well in home blenders and can be found in most supermarket freezers.

It's cold, it's wet, and it's always disappearing. But what's a summer drink without an ice cube? Have some fun with your kids concocting frosty, fruity, and flavored ice cubes to chill and change simple juices, iced teas, and even sparkling waters into extra-special drinks. First, get rid of all those old, stale, flat-tasting ice cubes that have spent the winter huddled together collecting freezer frost: Fill your preschooler's sand pail with a tray of ice cubes and set him or her free in the back yard to give your trees and outdoor plants a slow watering by placing the ice cubes around trees and sturdy plants. One tray at a time will prevent little fingers from getting too cold.

arctic treats

Just like North Pole explorers, kids can discover frozen surprises in the depths of an iceberg. First, buy fresh herbs and edible flowers or berries from your market's produce section. Some good choices are mint leaves, blueberries, raspberries, citrus flowers, scented geraniums, rose petals, pansies, or violets.

To make the ice cubes, fill the chambers in an ice-cube tray half full with water or herbal tea. Place in the freezer until the ice is mostly frozen, about 30 minutes. Meanwhile, gently rinse whatever you plan to freeze. When the ice is ready, place an edible treasure or two on the surface of each ice cube. Press lightly to make it stick or submerge slightly. Pour in more water to cover, then freeze.

sweet lemon zest ice cubes

Delicious in iced teas, lemonades, and juice drinks, these cubes are also fun to suck on by themselves. To make the ice cubes, combine 1 cup strained lemon juice and ½ cup sugar syrup. Fill an ice-cube tray two-thirds full with the mixture and freeze until almost frozen. For an extra touch, add a sliver of lemon zest with an edible blossom or petal to each chamber. Drizzle in more juice and freeze.

coffee ice cubes

Here is a great way for us big kids to cool off coffee drinks and colas: To make coffee ice cubes, brew regular-strength coffee using 2 level tablespoons freshly ground coffee or 2 teaspoons instant coffee granules for every 6 ounces (¾ cup) water. Let the coffee cool to room temperature before pouring it into ice-cube trays and freezing.

kaleidoscope kubes

Create special ice cubes by filling an ice-cube tray with all those "last of the juices." Anytime you have leftover juice, fill up the ice cube chambers and put the tray back in the freezer. On some hot afternoon when everybody's thirsty, set out a tray with clear plastic glasses, plain or flavored sparkling water, and a bowl of kaleidoscope kubes. Everyone can mix and match ice cubes and watch the colors blend and blur.

Summertime and the living is easy. . . *as easy as you can make it with summertime salads and finger-food snacks. Now's the chance to take a vacation and give your stove a rest. Make it a rule (well, maybe an excuse) never to go near the stove when the mercury rises. This is the season when farmers' markets and roadside stands can do the work for you. They have the freshest and tastiest*

summer salads and snacks

fruits and vegetables, so all you need is a flying stop for supermarket essentials and some quick and easy recipes.

Here you'll discover exotic fare cool enough to chill an Arabian night and easy enough for any teenage nomad to make on his own. You'll find a menu full of old-fashioned favorites like Roasted Greek Potato Salad and Dad's Favorite Deviled Eggs. Whenever a good book, a place in the shade, or a long-awaited visit is at hand, think of Gazpacho-to-Go or Black Bean and Corn Salsa Salad for a simple and quick summertime dish.

dad's favorite deviled eggs

12 eggs

³/₄ cup Miracle Whip salad
dressing or mayonnaise

4 teaspoons Dijon mustard

1 tablespoon fresh lemon juice

¹/₄ teaspoon kosher salt

Ground black pepper to taste

Fresh parsley leaves

I can't remember a summer picnic or party without deviled eggs made with Miracle Whip salad dressing. This is one of the first "party foods" I was allowed to fix by myself. Mom would hard-boil the eggs and I would do the rest, right down to filling the eggs and decorating them with a parsley leaf. You may want to use mayonnaise, but I'm sticking to my Dad's favorite dressing.

Serves 6

Place the eggs with cold water to cover in a large saucepan with a lid. Bring to a boil over medium-high heat. Immediately remove from heat, cover, and leave for 10 minutes. Drain off the hot water, and run the eggs under cold water until cool. Tap the eggs gently in several places to crack and then peel. (For easy peeling, place the cool eggs in a pan of cold water for 10 minutes before cracking.)

Slice the eggs in half lengthwise. Carefully remove the yolks from the whites, and place the yolks in a bowl. Add the salad dressing, mustard, lemon juice, salt, and pepper. Using a fork, mix until blended.

Refill the egg white halves with the yolk mixture, using a spoon or small spatula. Garnish with parsley leaves and chill thoroughly before serving.

deviled eggs ranchero

In a bowl, combine the yolks with ¹/₂ cup mayonnaise, ¹/₄ cup drained chunky hot salsa, ¹/₄ cup finely shredded Monterey Jack pepper or sharp Cheddar cheese, 2 tablespoons finely chopped fresh cilantro, and salt and ground black pepper to taste. Refill the egg whites. Garnish each with a dollop of guacamole and a sprinkling of finely minced fresh chives.

deviled caviar eggs

For this adult version, in a bowl, combine the yolks with $1/4$ cup mayonnaise, 1 teaspoon Dijon mustard, 2 teaspoons fresh lemon juice, 1 tablespoon finely minced fresh parsley, 2 teaspoons minced fresh chives, $1/8$ teaspoon hot pepper sauce, and 2 ounces caviar. Mix until blended. Season to taste with salt and ground black pepper. Refill the egg whites. Garnish each with a tiny dollop of sour cream and a dab of caviar. Serve with champagne.

black bean and corn salsa salad

While I was interviewing fitness expert Joe Piscatella about his book,
Fat-Proof Your Child, *he gave me a recipe for his wife's corn and black
bean salad. It reminded me of one I used to make the night before Pete
and I would hike to our farm's pond for a picnic and swim. Joe's recipe
had the zesty addition of jalapeño pepper and lime juice, so I tried it
with mine and now I have the best of two mouth-watering recipes.*

*Easy to put together and great with sandwiches, this colorful salad gets
better and better as it marinates in the refrigerator. If you're in a
hurry, don't worry if all you have is frozen corn. Just stir it in and let
it thaw. For your picnic, bring wedges of red and yellow sweet pepper
and serve your salad on them.*

Serves 6 to 8

To make the dressing, in a small bowl, whisk together the olive oil,
lime juice, garlic, cumin, and coriander until blended. Set aside for
30 minutes to let the flavors blend.

To make the salad, in a bowl, combine the black beans, corn, bell
peppers, jalapeños, and onion. Toss together gently. Pour the dressing
over the top and toss again. Add the tomato and gently toss again.
Cover and chill for several hours to let the flavors blend. Just before
serving, add the cilantro and toss well.

Notes: You can make the salad up to 2 days in advance. Do not add the
tomatoes until 1 to 3 hours before serving. To freshen the dressing,
squeeze lime juice to taste over the salad or make additional dressing.
Add the cilantro just before serving.

When handling fresh chiles, wear gloves. The volatile oils naturally
present in chiles can cause a burning sensation on your skin.

For the dressing

$1/3$ cup olive oil

$1/4$ cup fresh lime juice

1 clove garlic, minced

$1/2$ teaspoon ground cumin

$1/2$ teaspoon ground coriander

For the salad

2 cups freshly cooked black
beans, or 2 cans (15 ounces
each) rinsed and drained

2 cups corn kernels

1 small red bell pepper, seeded
and chopped ($3/4$ cup)

1 small orange bell pepper,
seeded and chopped ($3/4$ cup)

2 small jalapeño chiles, seeded
and finely minced (see note)

1 small sweet red or white
onion, finely chopped ($3/4$ cup)

1 large, ripe tomato, chopped

$1/2$ cup finely chopped fresh
cilantro or parsley

roasted greek potato salad

3 pounds new potatoes, unpeeled, quartered, or halved

1/4 cup olive oil, divided

1 red bell pepper, seeded and cut into 3/4-inch squares

1 yellow bell pepper, seeded and cut into 3/4-inch squares

1 head garlic, cloves separated and peeled

2 teaspoons minced fresh oregano leaves

1/4 cup fresh lemon juice

1/4 cup chopped fresh parsley

1/3 cup Kalamata olives, pitted and halved lengthwise

Salt and ground black pepper to taste

1/4 pound feta cheese, crumbled (about 1 cup)

Great with grilled meat or chicken, this hearty salad also makes a terrific main course when served with warm pita bread spread with flavored butters (page 71), fresh fruit, and followed with Yummy Ice Cream Sandwiches (page 84) for dessert. For an especially colorful presentation, serve on a platter or bowl lined with lettuce leaves.

Serves 6

Preheat a broiler. Position a rack 6 inches from the broiler element.

In a bowl, toss the potatoes with 2 tablespoons olive oil. Place the potatoes in a roasting pan, then slip under the broiler for 10 minutes. Remove from the broiler, add the red and yellow peppers, garlic cloves, and oregano, and toss to coat with the residual oil. Return to the broiler and cook, tossing all the vegetables every 5 minutes, until nicely browned and tender, about 15 minutes longer.

Remove from the broiler and transfer to a salad bowl. Drizzle with the remaining 2 tablespoons olive oil and the lemon juice and toss well. Let cool to room temperature. Add the parsley, olives, salt, and pepper and toss again.

Just before serving, toss in the feta cheese. Leftovers can be covered and refrigerated for up to 4 days. To freshen the salad, squeeze lemon juice to taste over the top and toss well.

iceberg wedges with blue cheese dressing

I've always liked iceberg lettuce. It's crisp, crunchy, and cool, and nothing could be simpler than iceberg wedges drizzled with your favorite dressing. If you like blue cheese, you'll love this dressing. Like me, you'll soon be using it as a dip for raw vegetables or as a spread on your favorite sandwich.

Serves 4 to 6

Discard any damaged outer leaves from the iceberg head, then rinse well and dry. Cut the head into 4 or 6 wedges and place on individual plates.

To make the dressing, in a food processor, blender, or with a handheld blender, combine the blue cheese, mayonnaise, sour cream, vinegar, lemon juice, garlic, green onions, parsley, salt, and pepper. Process until smooth. You should have about 1 3/4 cups.

Spoon 1/4 cup of the dressing over each wedge. Store any leftover dressing in a covered container in the refrigerator for up to 5 days.

1 head iceberg lettuce

For the dressing

2 to 3 ounces blue cheese, crumbled

1 cup mayonnaise

1/2 cup sour cream

2 tablespoons white wine vinegar

2 tablespoons fresh lemon juice

1 large clove garlic, mashed or crushed

2 green onions, chopped

1/4 cup Italian (flat-leaf) parsley leaves

1/4 teaspoon salt

1/8 teaspoon coarsely ground black pepper

tomato, mozzarella, and basil salad

4 large, ripe tomatoes, at room temperature

1 pound fresh mozzarella, sliced ¼ inch thick

¾ cup fresh basil leaves

Kosher or sea salt and ground black pepper to taste

1 to 4 tablespoons extra-virgin olive oil

Simple salads are sensational when the freshest, finest ingredients are used. My family likes this classic Italian salad dressed just with olive oil, but you can add balsamic vinegar or, if you're watching calories, use the vinegar by itself. Since the salad is composed of alternating layers of tomato, mozzarella, and basil leaves, it's an easy salad for the kids to help you make. Then they'll never forget the colors of Italy's national flag.

Serves 4

On 4 salad plates or on a serving platter, alternate slices of tomato and mozzarella with basil leaves. Season with salt and pepper. Drizzle olive oil over all and serve.

orange mint tabbouleh

Around our house, this naturally sweet summer salad has many lives. Freshly made, it complements a summer barbecue of grilled chicken and corn on the cob. When there are leftovers, we tuck them inside a warm pita bread pocket sandwich. Either way, it's divine.

Serves 4

To make the dressing, in a small bowl, whisk together the lemon juice, vinegar, mustard, olive oil, sugar, cinnamon, and cumin. Set aside.

In a medium bowl, combine the bulgur and boiling water. Let stand until the bulgur is light and fluffy, 30 to 45 minutes. Drain through a sieve and discard the water. Place the bulgur and 2 tablespoons dressing in another bowl and toss well. Let cool to room temperature.

Using a zester, remove the zest from the orange. Mince the zest and set aside. Cut the orange in half, squeeze enough juice to measure 3 tablespoons and place in a small glass bowl. Stir in the raisins and place in a microwave for 15 seconds to warm the juice. Remove from the microwave and let soak for 15 minutes.

Add the raisins and juice, orange zest, mint, parsley, green onions, celery, and remaining dressing to the bulgur mixture. Toss well and season with salt and pepper. Just before serving, toss in the mandarin oranges and chopped nuts and garnish with mint. Serve at room temperature.

Note: If you decide to chill the tabbouleh or serve it at a later time, the bulgur will absorb more of the dressing and the salad will need freshening. To do so, add 1 tablespoon orange juice or additional dressing and toss well.

For the dressing

$1/4$ cup fresh lemon juice

2 tablespoons white wine vinegar

$1^1/2$ teaspoons Dijon mustard

$1/3$ cup olive oil

1 teaspoon sugar

$1/4$ teaspoon ground cinnamon

$1/2$ teaspoon ground cumin

For the salad

1 cup bulgur, rinsed and drained

2 cups boiling water

1 orange

$1/3$ cup golden raisins

$1/4$ cup minced fresh mint leaves

$1/2$ cup minced fresh parsley leaves

4 green onions, chopped (about $1/4$ cup)

$1/2$ cup finely chopped celery

Salt and pepper to taste

$1/3$ cup mandarin orange segments

$1/3$ cup coarsely chopped nuts such as hazelnuts or cashews

Tiny mint sprigs for garnish

gazpacho-to-go

A quick version of a fresh summer classic—and one that your teenagers can make for you—this chilled tomato-vegetable soup looks especially pretty served in clear glass mugs. If you're taking it on a picnic, pack the soup in a clear storage container to show off its mosaic of colors, and be sure to keep it well chilled in your cooler.

Serves 4 to 6

In a large bowl, whisk together the vinegar, olive oil, sugar, dill, garlic, Tabasco sauce, and vegetable juice until blended. (The recipe can be made ahead to this point and chilled overnight.) Stir in the cherry tomatoes, cucumber, onion, yellow pepper, and cream cheese. Cover and chill thoroughly.

To serve, ladle into chilled clear glass mugs or bowls and garnish with the avocado and cilantro.

variation

Stir in 1/4 pound cooked baby shrimp before serving. Substitute other tomato-based vegetable juices such as those containing clam broth.

2 tablespoons red wine vinegar

2 tablespoons extra-virgin olive oil

2 teaspoons sugar

1 teaspoon dried dill

2 cloves garlic, minced

1/4 teaspoon Tabasco or other hot pepper sauce

4 cups (1 quart) vegetable juice such as V-8

1 cup halved yellow or red cherry tomatoes

1/2 cup peeled, seeded, and chopped cucumber

1/4 cup chopped red onion

1/2 cup seeded and chopped yellow bell pepper

3 ounces cream cheese, diced

1 ripe avocado, pitted, peeled, and sliced or diced

1/4 cup snipped fresh cilantro (optional)

Imagine a long and beautiful trail that winds from Memorial Day to Labor Day. Along the way comes Flag Day on June 14, followed by Father's Day on the third Sunday in June, and the Fourth of July. There's so much to do: picnics in the park, backyard barbecues, trips to the pool, Sunday brunch for Mom just because she's special.

summer celebrations

Start a summer morning with Sweet Mama's Morning Cakes and Melon–Lemon Sorbet Compote. At noon, enjoy a Super Sub Sandwich long enough to feed a softball team. Warm evenings are just right for Dad's special Grilled Flank Steak with its sizzling charcoal flavor and savory mustard rub. Host a fantastic Fourth of July bash with a savory Mixed Summer Grill and Corn on the Cob with Flavored Butters. In this chapter you'll find menus and recipes for a Memorial Day Tailgate Picnic, a Sunny Sunday Patio Brunch, a Father's Day Barbecue, and a Fourth of July Star-Spangled Celebration. All of these fantastic menus are designed to keep you out of the kitchen as much as possible so you can get out and enjoy the great outdoors. Happy trails to you!

super sub sandwich

2 oblong loaves French or
sourdough bread

Olive oil for drizzling

1/2 to 1 cup flavored butters
(page 71) or purchased olive
spread

Salt and ground black pepper

1/3 pound (20 thin slices) cheese
such as Swiss or Jack

1/3 pound (26 thin slices) cold-cut
meats such as ham or turkey

4 cups lettuce leaves

4 to 6 tomatoes, thinly sliced

2 red onions, thinly sliced

2 red bell peppers, seeded and
thinly sliced

1 jar (16 ounces) pepperoncini
peppers, drained

1/4 cup chopped fresh oregano

1/2 cup fresh basil leaves

Because of its length, this sandwich lets you switch the fillings several times, guaranteeing that even the pickiest eater will be satisfied. To gauge your cuts, plant a skewer where each filling starts.

Serves 10 to 12

Cut the heels from each loaf, then cut each loaf in half horizontally, making the bottom halves slightly larger.

Scoop out some of the soft bread from the bottom halves. Place the loaves end to end on a long tray or board. Drizzle the olive oil over the bottom halves, and spread with flavored butters or olive spread. Begin covering the bottom halves, treating them as 1 large loaf, with your choices of thin, repeating layers of cheeses, meats, vegetables, and herbs. Drizzle the top halves of the bread with olive oil, salt, and pepper. Place the tops on the sandwiches and press down firmly.

To serve, cut into 3/4-inch-wide strips. Poke long toothpicks through each strip so that the pieces don't separate. If you're making the sandwich in advance, treat the 2 loaves separately, wrap them tightly in plastic wrap, and refrigerate until 1 hour before serving time.

memorial day tailgate picnic menu

Gazpacho-to-Go (page 59), Super Sub Sandwich,

Black Bean and Corn Salsa Salad (page 53), sliced watermelon,

Chocolate Spanish Peanut Cookies (page 84),

Blue-Ribbon Berry Parfaits (page 86), assorted frozen candy bars,

soft drinks, draft beer, and coffee

melon–lemon sorbet compote

1 teaspoon rose water (optional)

1 cup cantaloupe balls

1 cup honeydew melon balls

1 cup seedless watermelon balls

1 pint lemon sorbet

Mint leaves for garnish

sunny sunday patio brunch menu

Melon-Lemon Sorbet Compote

Sweet Mama's Morning Cakes (page 67)

Toasted Pecan Honey Butter (page 67) or Strawberry Sauce (page 75)

Crisp bacon or sausage patties

Orange juice

Coffee or herbal tea

The kids can help you form the melon and sorbet balls, although they'll probably eat more than they make. When you serve the compote, tell your kids not to eat all the sorbet balls first. As the lemony ice melts, it makes a terrific instant sauce.

Serves 4 to 6

Pour the rose water, if using, into a medium bowl. Tilt and turn the bowl to coat the sides and bottom. Discard any surplus. Add the cantaloupe, honeydew, and watermelon balls and toss gently. Cover and chill for 1 to 2 hours.

Meanwhile, let the sorbet sit out for 10 minutes if frozen solid. Make room in your freezer for a baking sheet. Using a ¾-inch melon-baller, form sorbet balls and place them on the baking sheet. Place the sheet in the freezer and freeze until firm, about 30 minutes.

To serve, add the sorbet balls to the melon mixture and toss gently. Spoon into stemmed glasses. Garnish with mint leaves.

quick and simple centerpieces

Here are a few ideas for making a table centerpiece as special as the menu: Tuck garden flowers and herb sprigs inside a chintzware teapot or pitcher. Fill a glass goblet or vase with colorful layers of sand and shells to create a candleholder for dripless tapers. Ask your kids to pick a few flowers from the garden, and then float the blossoms in an attractive yet simple bowl filled with water. Place several plant-filled Sponge-Painted Patio Pots (page 19) on a round brass tray.

sweet mama's morning cakes

These pancakes are firm enough to hold like toast and young eaters who don't want to use forks and knives can make pancake rollups. With a little help from a teenager or grown-up, your kids can have fun using their creative flair to make Smiling Baby Cakes with grins.

Serves 4 to 6

In a large bowl, combine the flour, sugar, baking powder, and salt. In a small bowl, stir together the eggs, milk, and oil. Pour the egg mixture into the flour mixture and mix until smooth. Set aside.

Coat an electric skillet or griddle with cooking spray and preheat to 350°F for 5 minutes. (This is a lower temperature than conventional pancakes use.) Working in batches, pour 1/4 cup batter onto the hot griddle for each cake. Cook until the top is bubbly and the cake is dry around the edges. Flip over and cook until golden on the second side.

Serve the cakes warm or at room temperature with the toasted pecan honey butter and strawberry sauce.

toasted pecan honey butter

Preheat oven to 350°F. Spread 1/3 cup pecans in a pan, and bake until lightly toasted, 5 to 8 minutes. Let cool and chop finely. In a bowl, beat together 1/2 cup (1 stick) unsalted butter and 1/4 cup honey until combined. Stir in the pecans. Serve at room temperature.

smiling baby cakes

Use 1 tablespoon batter to first outline a smile and two dots for eyes on the heated griddle. Once the batter begins to bubble and dry, pour 1/4 cup batter around the eyes and smile and fill in.

1 1/2 cups all-purpose flour

3/4 cup sugar

1 1/4 teaspoons baking powder

1/2 teaspoon salt

2 eggs

1 cup milk

2 tablespoons salad oil

Toasted pecan honey butter (recipe below)

Strawberry sauce (page 75)

67

grilled flank steak

1 flank steak, 1½ to 2 pounds

For the mustard rub

¼ cup prepared Dijon mustard

2 teaspoons dry mustard

2 teaspoons garlic salt

1 teaspoon coarsely ground
black pepper

For the sauce

2 tablespoons unsalted butter,
melted

1 tablespoon finely minced fresh
Italian (flat-leaf) parsley

2 teaspoons fresh lemon juice

1 clove garlic, minced

*father's day
barbecue menu*

Grilled Flank Steak

Mixed green salad

Five-Spice Peach Blueberry
Crisp (page 93)

Sunshine Tea (page 36), beer,
and coffee

Father's Day dinner is always the same at our house: flank steak on the barbecue. It's always the centerpiece, although the side dishes may change from year to year. Even when Matthew and Julie were young, they loved the salty mustard rub and the sauce we drizzled over their meat. I think you'll find this steak a winner with your family, too.

Serves 4 to 6

With a sharp knife, lightly score the flank steak on both sides. This will keep it from curling during grilling.

To make the mustard rub, in a small bowl, combine the prepared and dry mustards, garlic salt, and pepper and stir to make a paste. Place the steak in a shallow dish or pan. Rub half of the mustard mixture into the topside of the meat, making sure the paste penetrates the scored areas. Marinate at room temperature for 35 to 40 minutes.

Preheat a fire in a charcoal grill, or preheat a gas grill. Place a cutting board with ridges that slant toward the center to concentrate the juices inside a large serving platter.

To make the sauce, in a small bowl or pitcher, combine the butter, parsley, lemon juice, and garlic and mix well. Set aside.

Place the steak, mustard side down, on the grill rack over a medium-hot fire. Smooth the remaining paste on the top side. Grill, turning once, until done, 5 to 7 minutes on each side for medium-rare or as desired. Remove the grilled steak to the cutting board. Drizzle the butter sauce over the meat. Using a sharp knife, thinly slice on the diagonal. Spoon the juices over the meat and serve buffet-style.

fourth of july star-spangled celebration

Hands down, the Fourth of July is the biggest and best summer holiday. It's a day of family reunions and yearly traditions that become more delicious and meaningful with each generation. It's starting your own tradition with your favorite sizzling barbecue, corn on the cob, and America's best strawberry shortcake. It's hanging Uncle Mark's 1956 souvenir flag from a pole, a porch, or a window. It's the day to create your own extended family with friends and neighbors or a homesick colleague.

Anticipating the day makes it even more fun, especially with crafts and projects that everyone can make. Rainy days in June all but disappear when beaming kids surround the kitchen table, deeply absorbed in the busy work of stamping stars and painting stripes. On the big day, you and your kids will feel the same button-bursting pride as the early patriots when they waved their star-spangled banners.

fourth of july barbecue menu

Dad's Favorite Deviled Eggs (page 50)

A Mixed Summer Grill (page 70)

Grilled Corn on the Cob with Flavored Butters (page 71)

Clare's Potato Salad (page 73)

Fresh Strawberry Shortcake with Summer Cream (page 75)

Bianca's Extra-Lemony Sidewalk Lemonade (page 37)

Lime Fizz (page 39)

a mixed summer grill

For the marinade

¹⁄₄ cup virgin olive oil

¹⁄₄ cup roasted peanut, hazelnut, or walnut oil

2 teaspoons kosher salt

2 teaspoons medium-grind black pepper

6 large cloves garlic

¹⁄₂ cup fresh lemon juice

6 to 8 drumsticks or 2 boneless chicken breast halves, about 1 pound total weight

2 loin lamb chops, about ³⁄₄ pound total weight and 1 inch thick

1 salmon steak, about ³⁄₄ pound and 1¹⁄₂ inches thick

2 Italian sausages, or your kid's favorite style, about ¹⁄₂ pound total weight

Vegetable oil for grill rack

This is the closest thing to a universal marinade. My family likes it on every kind of meat and seafood, although chicken is our favorite.

Serves 6

To make the marinade, in a small bowl, combine the olive oil, peanut oil, salt, pepper, garlic, and lemon juice.

Place the drumsticks, lamb chops, salmon, and sausages in 1 or 2 shallow pans large enough to hold them in a single layer. Pour the marinade over the top, and turn the pieces to coat both sides. Cover and refrigerate for 1 hour or as long as overnight, turning several times.

If using hardwood chips—cherry, apple, hickory, mesquite—soak them in water to cover for at least an hour or until they sink, so the chips smoke instead of burn.

Oil the rack of a charcoal or gas grill. Prepare a fire or preheat the grill. When the fire is ready, drain the chips and add to the charcoal grill 5 minutes before adding the chicken. If using a gas grill, wrap the drained chips in aluminum foil, poke a few holes in the foil, and place under the cooking grates on top of the gas fire.

Remove the meat from the marinade. Place the drumsticks on the grill rack and sear on all sides. Continue to grill until cooked, 5 to 7 minutes. (Chicken breasts are cooked when an instant-read thermometer inserted into the thickest part reads 175 degrees.) Grill the lamb chops, salmon, and sausage alongside the chicken, turning as necessary. Allow about 4 minutes on each side for the chops for medium-rare, 5 to 6 minutes on each side for the salmon, and a total of 8 to 10 minutes for the sausages, or until nearly charred. Remove from the grill rack and let rest for several minutes before serving.

grilled corn on the cob
with flavored butters

Kids can have a good time helping you get the corn ready for grilling. The flavored butters are a tasty accompaniment to vegetables, meats, seafood, and bread.

12 young tender ears of corn

Flavored butters (recipes follow)

Serves 6

Carefully pull the husks back on each ear, but don't tear them off. Pull out the corn silk and discard. Pull the husks back over each ear, and tie securely near the tip with a torn strip of corn husk or kitchen string. Soak the prepared ears of corn in a basin of water for 1 hour. This will keep the husks from burning on the grill.

Prepare a fire in a charcoal grill, or preheat a gas grill. Place the corn on the grill rack over medium-low fire and grill, turning often, until cooked, 15 to 20 minutes. To check for doneness, remove 1 ear, pull back the husk, and pierce a kernel with the tip of a knife. The juice should be milky.

Remove from the grill and serve immediately with one or more of the flavored butters.

tarragon butter

In a bowl, using a handheld blender or fork, combine 1/2 cup (1 stick) unsalted butter (at room temperature), 1 tablespoon chopped fresh tarragon, 2 teaspoons Dijon mustard, and 1/4 teaspoon salt until blended. Spoon the butter onto a piece of plastic wrap, and shape it into a small sausage. Wrap tightly and refrigerate until firm. For longer storage, wrap a second time in foil. To use as a sauce, slice off a round and let it melt on the hot food. To use as a spread, let the butter warm to room temperature. Use on hot vegetables, grilled chicken, and fish. Makes 1/2 cup.

grilling tips

* To keep meat and fish from sticking, your grill must be clean and hot.

* To test the temperature of the fire, place your hand over the ash-white coals, about 1 inch above the rack, and count to three, using the "one-one thousand" style.

* Just before laying the food on the rack, wipe the rack from the back to the front with a clean rag dipped in vegetable oil. (If you go from front to back, you might lose some hair on your arm.)

continued on next page

roasted garlic butter

Preheat an oven to 450°F. Remove the papery outer layers from a large garlic head. Cut off about ½ inch from the top of the head and discard. Place the head in the center of a 10-inch square of aluminum foil. Drizzle with olive oil. Wrap the garlic in the foil and twist the top to seal. Bake until the pulp is soft, about 20 minutes. Remove from the oven, let cool, and squeeze the pulp from the garlic cloves into a small bowl. Add ½ cup (1 stick) unsalted butter (at room temperature), 1 teaspoon fresh lemon juice, and ½ teaspoon salt. Proceed as directed in the Tarragon Butter recipe. This is delicious on everything. Makes ½ cup.

chile lime butter

Remove the seeds from a small ancho chile. (Ancho chiles can be found in Latin American markets and well-stocked supermarkets.) Wear rubber gloves when handling any chiles because the volatile oils can cause a burning sensation on your skin. Place the chiles in warm water to cover for 5 minutes to soften. Drain, and mince almost to a paste. (This can leave a stubborn stain on your cutting board, so wash the board immediately.) Reserve ½ teaspoon paste for the butter. Discard the rest, or wrap tightly and freeze for another recipe.

In a small bowl, using a handheld blender or fork, combine ½ cup (1 stick) unsalted butter (at room temperature), the grated zest of 1 lime, and the reserved minced chile until blended. (For more spice, add a dash of cayenne pepper.) Proceed as directed in the Tarragon Butter recipe. This is delicious on corn, grilled fish, and chicken. Makes ½ cup.

clare's potato salad

My friend Bette Sinclair gave me this quintessential potato salad recipe. Her mother-in-law, Clare, would fix this salad when the family came for Sunday supper. Clare, who was born in San Francisco in 1894, said the recipe had belonged to her mother, and that it had gone a long way toward feeding Clare and her seven brothers and sisters. While your family may not be as large as Clare's, they will want this crunchy, creamy, old-fashioned salad as a regular feature at any gathering.

Serves 8

In a 4-quart Dutch oven, place the potatoes and add water to cover. Bring to a boil, reduce the heat to a simmer, and cook, uncovered, until tender, 20 to 25 minutes. Drain and let cool for 10 minutes.

Peel the potatoes while they are still warm. Cut into bite-size pieces and place them in a large bowl. Drizzle with the vinegar, dust with table salt, and toss well.

Remove the yolks from 3 eggs; reserve the whites. With a fork or handheld blender, combine the 3 yolks, the mayonnaise, lemon juice, and mustard until smooth. Stir in the onion. Pour the dressing over the potatoes and toss. Add the celery, parsley, capers, and half of the chives and toss well. Chop the reserved whites and the remaining 3 eggs, add them to the salad, and toss again. Season with kosher salt and pepper to taste. Cover and refrigerate for 2 hours to blend the flavors, stirring occasionally.

Line individual plates with butter leaves and spoon the salad onto them. Dust with paprika and sprinkle with the remaining chives. Serve at once.

2½ pounds Yellow Finn potatoes (about 8), unpeeled

¼ cup apple cider vinegar

Table salt to taste

6 hard-boiled eggs, peeled and divided

1 cup mayonnaise

2½ to 3 tablespoons fresh lemon juice

1½ tablespoons Dijon mustard

½ cup chopped red onion

3 large celery stalks, some with leaves intact, chopped

2 tablespoons chopped Italian (flat-leaf) parsley

2 tablespoons drained small capers

2 tablespoons minced fresh chives, divided

Kosher salt and ground white pepper to taste

Butter lettuce leaves

Paprika for dusting

fresh strawberry shortcake
with summer cream

Our Fourth of July party isn't complete without this classic American summer dessert. We serve it buffet style and let everyone make their own. If you have other fresh berries, go ahead and make a medley to top the shortcakes. And, if you have kids itching for a project, let them make Shake-Rattle-and-Roll Ice Cream (page 90) to top it off.

For those who are worried about calories and fat, substitute chilled or frozen low-fat lemon or vanilla yogurt.

Serves 6 to 8

Place the strawberries in a bowl and sweeten with granulated sugar to taste. Set aside.

To make the strawberry sauce, in a food processor, combine the strawberries, powdered sugar, and lemon juice. Puree until smooth. Set aside for 30 minutes. Makes about $2^2/_3$ cups.

Preheat an oven to 425°F.

To make the shortcakes, in a large bowl, stir together the flour, granulated sugar, baking powder, and salt. Add the butter and cut it in with a pastry blender until the mixture resembles coarse crumbs. Do not overmix. The bits of butter should still be cool to the touch. Combine the milk and vanilla, and stir into the flour mixture until a dough begins to form.

2 pints fresh strawberries, hulled and sliced

Granulated sugar for sweetening

For the strawberry sauce

2 pints strawberries, hulled and sliced

$^3/_4$ cup powdered sugar

2 teaspoons fresh lemon juice

For the shortcakes

2 cups all-purpose flour

2 tablespoons sugar

1 tablespoon baking powder

$^1/_2$ teaspoon salt

$^1/_2$ cup chilled unsalted butter, cut into pieces

$^2/_3$ cup milk

1 teaspoon vanilla extract

continued on next page

For the summer cream

1 cup heavy cream

1 tablespoon sugar

1 teaspoon rose water (optional; see note)

½ cup strawberry sauce

Dust your hands with flour, and loosely gather and squeeze together the dough. Turn it out onto a lightly floured surface. Knead gently two or three times. Pat out the dough 1 inch thick. Using a biscuit or cookie cutter, 2½ inches in diameter, or a knife, cut out 6 to 8 shortcakes. Place on an ungreased baking sheet. Bake until golden, 10 to 12 minutes.

Meanwhile, make the summer cream: In a bowl, whip the cream until soft peaks form. Add the sugar and rose water, if using, and continue to whip until stiff peaks just begin to form. Fold the ½ cup strawberry sauce into the whipped cream ¼ cup at a time, using a rubber spatula to make a swirling pattern. Leave some "ribbons" of sauce visible.

Remove the shortcakes from the oven and let cool briefly. Split each warm shortcake in half, and spread 1 to 2 tablespoons sauce over the cut sides. Spoon the sliced strawberries over the cakes, dividing evenly. Cover with the remaining sauce and top with the summer cream. Serve at once.

Note: Rose water is available at most supermarkets in the condiment section. It is also available where liquor is sold. If unavailable, substitute vanilla or another favorite pure flavoring extract.

stars and stripes dinnerware

Water-based acrylic paints make this project good for everyone in the family. Any mistakes can simply be washed away. The plates shown on page 79 have a random pattern that little patriots can stamp all by themselves. Follow the directions to create star-spangled place settings you can mix and match.

Makes four 4-piece place settings

Cover a flat, clutter-free work surface with long sheets of waxed paper so that they overlap by 2 inches. Make sure the paper towels and moist sponge are within easy reach for quick cleanups.

To make the stamps, scrub the potato with warm water and dry with paper towels, pressing the potato skin firmly to remove any excess moisture. With the knife, slice the potato in half crosswise, and blot the cut ends dry with a paper towel. Position the smaller star cookie cutter in the center of a potato half, and score around each side to a $1/2$-inch depth. Remove the cookie cutter. Cut in on each side to meet the scored edges. Pull the cut pieces away, leaving the star stamp in the center. Repeat this process on the other half using the larger star cookie cutter. Set the completed stamps aside on a double fold of paper towel.

Pour about 1 tablespoon blue paint into one of the plastic lids. Dip the smaller star stamp into the paint, and stamp a few practice stars onto scratch paper to get a feel for the technique. Select the first salad plate, and set it upside down on the waxed paper. (You will be stamping the outside bottom of the plate.)

Dip the stamp in the paint and position it over the rim of the plate where you want the star to be. Carefully stamp the first star. To avoid smearing, lift the stamp straight up, without moving it to the left

Waxed paper

Paper towels

Kitchen sponge

1 firm russet potato, 3 inches in diameter

Sharp paring knife

$1^{1}/_{2}$-inch star-shaped cookie cutter

$2^{1}/_{2}$-inch star-shaped cookie cutter

1 bottle (2 ounces) navy blue water-soluble acrylic paint

2 plastic lids for paint, each 4 inches in diameter

White scratch paper

4 clear glass salad plates

1 bottle (2 ounces) bright red water-soluble acrylic paint

4 clear glass dinner plates

Clear acrylic spray

4 clear glass bowls

Round-tipped paintbrush, $1/_{4}$ inch wide

4 clear glass beverage glasses

continued on next page

or right. Continue stamping around the rim of the plate, leaving about $\frac{1}{2}$ inch between the stars. Repeat with the remaining salad plates. Using the larger star, the red paint, and the second plastic lid, apply the same technique on the dinner plates. Let the paint dry thoroughly.

Once the paint is dry, set the design: Apply a coat of clear acrylic spray to the painted side of each plate. This makes the design permanent.

To paint the bowls and glasses, using the paintbrush, make a series of small red dots in a straight line on the outside of each bowl, 1 inch below the rim. Then connect the dots to make a stripe around the bowl. The step can be repeated to make a double stripe or a thicker stripe, but you must allow the outline stripe to dry first so that it doesn't smear. Repeat for each bowl and glass.

This dinnerware should be washed by hand from now on.

variation

Why stop at place settings? Try your hand at decorating serving platters, bowls, and other tableware.

checkerboard star
picnic tablecloth

Disposable plastic drop cloth

White fabric or plastic picnic tablecloth, desired shape and size

Masking tape

Paper towels

Kitchen sponge

1 firm russet potato, 3 inches in diameter

Sharp paring knife

1½-inch star-shaped cookie cutter

1 bottle (2 ounces) bright red acrylic fabric paint

2 plastic lids for paint, each 4 inches in diameter

Plain white scratch paper

1 bottle (2 ounces) navy blue acrylic fabric paint

Whether you're planning a Fourth of July family reunion or a neighborhood get-together, here's a craft for everyone. While you may want to do a particular pattern on the tablecloth, the kids can show their artistic talent by scattering stars and squares over plain white napkins, T-shirts, or aprons. Don't forget the babies in the family. Blue stars and red checks make a plain white one-piece romper or bib look very festive.

Makes 1 picnic tablecloth

Cover a large, flat work surface with the plastic drop cloth. Spread the tablecloth on top of it, smoothing out any folds or wrinkles. Using masking tape, mark the borders of the areas you wish to print on the cloth. This can be a symmetrical border or a confetti of images throughout the cloth. Make sure the paper towels and kitchen sponge are within easy reach for quick cleanups.

To make the star stamp, proceed as directed in Stars and Stripes Dinnerware (see page 77).

To make a square stamp, score a 1½-inch square into the flat side of a potato half to a ½-inch depth. Cut in on each side to meet the scored edges.

Pour about 1 tablespoon red paint into one of the plastic lids. Dip the square potato stamp into the paint, and stamp a few practice squares onto the scratch paper to get a feel for the technique. Begin to stamp on the picnic cloth. Work from one side to the other, beginning at the farthest point and working toward yourself, being careful not to stamp on the masking tape. Let the paint dry, before repeating the same process with the blue paint and star pattern. Let the picnic cloth dry completely before removing the masking tape, and moving it.

red, white, and blue parade wand

Red, white, and blue ribbon streamers make it easy for a child to fly America's colors high. Have your own front porch parade with these easy-to-make, festive wands.

Makes 1 wand

Cover a flat, clutter-free work surface with long sheets of waxed paper so that they overlap by 2 inches. Holding one end of the dowel, paint the other half on all sides with the red paint. Stand the unpainted end in a soda bottle, and let the paint dry completely, 10 to 20 minutes. When dry, hold the dowel's painted end and paint the remaining half, allowing it to dry, wet end up, in the soda bottle.

Lay the 9 lengths of red, white, and blue ribbon together, alternating them so there is an even balance of color. Gather the ribbons up by one end and, using a 4- to 6-inch piece of masking tape, attach them to what will be the top 2 to 3 inches of the streamer wand. It is important to keep the ribbon smooth, and the tape secure. Apply a thick line of glue to the top 3 inches of the wand, drawing it on top of the masking tape. Center one of the paper stars over the glue line, and secure the star by holding it in place until the glue has set. On the reverse side, line the points of the second star up with the points of the first star, and repeat the gluing process.

Note: If you don't have a glue gun or little fingers are tackling this project on their own, a craft glue or white glue can be used.

Waxed paper

3-foot wooden dowel, $\frac{1}{4}$ inch thick

Flat-edged paintbrush, $\frac{1}{2}$ inch wide

1 bottle (2 ounces) bright red craft paint

Soda bottle

2 yards red satin ribbon, $\frac{1}{8}$ inch wide, cut into three 2-foot lengths

2 yards white satin ribbon, $\frac{1}{8}$ inch wide, cut into three 2-foot lengths

2 yards blue satin ribbon, $\frac{1}{8}$ inch wide, cut into three 2-foot lengths

Masking tape

Hot glue gun or craft glue (see note)

2 stars, each 4 inches wide, cut from blue construction paper

Summertime treats always include summertime sweets. Plump fruits and ripe berries wrapped in sweet cream and buttery short cake. The ultimate soft and chunky chocolate cookie studded with Spanish peanuts and chocolate chips.

summer sweets

Homemade ice cream that's as much fun to make as it is to eat—all you need is a handful of kids with lots of shake-rattle-and-roll. Hold an ice cream social and satisfy a whole neighborhood's sweet tooth. Experience the simple pleasure of shaping, stuffing, and nibbling a healthful, no-bake candy with your favorite preschooler. Create a baroque Blue-Ribbon Berry Parfait that makes any summer party a sophisticated soiree. Only you will know how easy it is to make.

chocolate spanish peanut cookies

2/3 cup unsalted butter, softened

1 cup sugar

2 eggs

1 teaspoon vanilla extract

1 cup all-purpose flour

1/2 cup cocoa

1/2 teaspoon baking soda

1 teaspoon salt

1 cup semisweet chocolate chips

1/2 cup Spanish peanuts

more chocolate?

It's easy. Let your kids decorate the cookies by filling a sealable, 1-pint freezer bag with 2/3 cup semisweet chocolate chips and 2 teaspoons vegetable oil. Microwave on high until the chips are soft, about 1 minute. Knead the bag to blend the chips and oil. Snip a tiny opening in a bottom corner of the bag, and let the kids squeeze the chocolate over the cookies.

We first tasted these delicious cookies on the beach during a family vacation. They were baked by Lisa Allen, the owner of the Pacific Way Bakery & Cafe in Gearhart, Oregon. Once the vacation was over, Matthew and Julie kept asking if I would make the same kind of cookie with Spanish peanuts. With a few minor changes, here's the recipe. This cookie also makes great ice cream sandwiches.

Makes 1 1/2 dozen

Preheat the oven to 350° F. Have ready 2 baking sheets.

In a bowl, combine the butter and sugar and, using an electric mixer, beat until light and creamy. Beat in the eggs and vanilla and continue to mix for 2 minutes.

In another bowl, stir together the flour, cocoa, baking soda, and salt. Gradually stir the flour mixture into the butter mixture. Stir in the chocolate chips and nuts. Drop by tablespoonfuls onto a baking sheet, leaving 2 inches between each mound of dough. Bake until set, 10 to 12 minutes. Let cool for several minutes on the baking sheets before transferring to a wire rack. The cookies will be soft and chewy.

yummy ice cream sandwiches

Omit the Spanish peanuts and chocolate chips and bake for 12 to 14 minutes. The cookies will be firm and turn out as perfect circles. Choose a pint of your favorite ice cream—my family loves peppermint—and remove it from its container. Cut the ice cream into slices, and sandwich each slice between 2 cookies. Or use the scoop-and-squish method for the ice-cream centers.

silver s'mores

Here's a quick idea for everyone's favorite summer campfire treat. This time, though, there are no messy sticks or dripping marshmallows. I like to surprise the kids by assembling the s'mores ahead of time and bringing them out just before we start dessert. No matter how old they are, they come running once they spy those silver packets.

Serves 6

Prepare a fire in a covered charcoal grill, or preheat a gas grill.

Top a cracker square with half a candy bar, a marshmallow, and another cracker. Repeat until the six s'mores are assembled. Place one s'more in the middle of an 8-by-12-inch sheet of aluminum foil. Bring up the sides and seal, leaving room inside the packet for heat to circulate. Repeat with the remaining ingredients to create 6 packets in all.

Place the packets on the grill, positioning them near the edges where it's cooler. Cover and heat the packets until the marshmallows are melted, 4 to 5 minutes. It's a good idea to test one packet to make sure the fire is not too hot. If it is, the crackers will burn. If it's too cold, the chocolate will melt but the marshmallow won't. The aluminum foil cools fairly fast, so that older kids can open the packets themselves. It's best to help kids under 6, by partially opening the packets to make sure the contents are not too hot.

6 graham crackers, each
2½ by 5 inches, divided in
half crosswise

3 milk chocolate candy bars,
each about 1½ ounces,
divided in half crosswise

6 large marshmallows

is it raining outside?

You can still enjoy a gooey s'more. Instead of a marshmallow, use marshmallow cream and forget the foil. Slip it in the microwave just long enough to melt the chocolate. Yum, yum.

blue-ribbon berry parfaits

1 pint raspberries

1 pint blueberries

Sugar for sweetening

1½ cups chilled heavy cream

1½ cups purchased or
homemade lemon curd,
at room temperature

3 cups gingersnap or coconut
macaroon broken cookies or
cookie crumbs

These pretty desserts will travel far beyond your dining room table if you make them in clear plastic cups. An 8- to 10-ounce cup works perfectly for each parfait. Kids can help measure and pour and create the different layers. Once they get the knack, they'll want to make the breakfast version for an afternoon snack.

Serves 6

Chill a bowl and beater blades.

In another bowl, combine the raspberries and blueberries and sweeten with sugar if necessary.

In the chilled bowl, whip the cream until soft peaks begin to form. Add the lemon curd and continue to beat until blended and soft peaks form.

To assemble each parfait, place ¼ cup cookie crumbs into a clear plastic (or glass) cup. Top with ¼ cup mixed berries and then ¼ cup whipped cream mixture. Repeat the layers, then top with a layer of berries and a dollop of whipped cream. Chill for 1 to 4 hours.

If you are transporting the parfaits, seal each plastic cup with plastic wrap and keep chilled in a cooler.

breakfast berry parfaits

Substitute granola for the gingersnaps and lemon yogurt for the lemon curd and whipped cream.

fresh fruit cookie pie

This sugar cookie pie is an easy dessert for kids to make and decorate. To celebrate Flag Day on June 14, let the kids shape the dough on a rectangular baking pan and make a giant American flag cookie (see below), using blueberries and red berries for decoration. Or, why not have them design a flag just for the family?

Serves 6 to 8

Preheat an oven to 350°F. Lightly grease a 12-inch pizza pan.

With clean hands, let the kids press the dough to fit the pan as evenly as possible. (Don't worry if it's a little uneven.) Crimp the edges and prick the surface with the tines of a fork. Bake until the dough begins to brown all over, about 10 minutes. Let cool on a wire rack.

In a medium bowl, combine the cream cheese, sour cream, powdered sugar, vanilla, lemon zest, and half-and-half. Stir until smooth. Spread evenly over the cooled cookie crust.

To decorate, arrange the strawberries, blueberries, grapes, and raspberries in your own design. Slice the cookie pizza in wedges and enjoy.

star-spangled cookie

Proceed as directed, but bake in a 13-by-9-by-2-inch baking pan instead of a pizza pan. Spread the cream cheese mixture on the cookie. To make a traditional American flag, line up the blueberries to create a 3-by-5-inch blue field in the upper left-hand corner. Arrange the sliced strawberries or raspberries to create the red stripes. The white frosting represents the white stripes.

1 package (18 ounces) refrigerator sugar cookie dough

1 package (8 ounces) cream cheese, at room temperature

2 tablespoons sour cream

2 to 4 tablespoons powdered sugar

2 teaspoons vanilla extract

1 teaspoon minced lemon zest (optional)

1 tablespoon half-and-half

1 pint strawberries, hulled and sliced

1 pint blueberries

1 cup seedless grapes

1 pint raspberries

neighborhood ice cream sundae

Have an ice cream social in your backyard. The set up is easy and it's a cool way for kids and parents to be together.

Serves 10 to 12

To prepare the ice cream, remove the ice cream from the cartons several hours or the day before the party, and cut each block into 1-inch-thick slices. Place the slices between pieces of waxed paper, and repack or store in plastic bags in the freezer.

To prepare the sundaes, first set up the table: Run sheets of aluminum foil the length of the two tables. Fold up the edges of the foil to form side walls. You will now have 1 giant tray covering each table. (For easy cleanup when the party is over, roll up the foil and toss.)

Warm the fudge, chocolate, and caramel sauces, and pour them into separate small pitchers. To dilute the marshmallow cream to a pouring consistency, place the open jar in the microwave and heat it for 15 to 20 seconds. Stir with a spoon so the warm, puffy cream deflates, then stir in enough half-and-half to achieve the proper consistency. Pour into a small pitcher.

Place the walnuts, peanuts, almonds, and sliced strawberries in separate bowls.

Just before serving time, gather up your family of helpers to place the ice cream slices lengthwise down the center of the foil "tray." Put the pitchers, bowls, and decorative sprinkles along the length of the tray and the bananas alongside the slices of ice cream. Pass the cherries and spoons, and see how many different sundae combinations you and your family and friends can create.

3 half-gallon cartons ice cream in your favorite flavors

1½ cups homemade or purchased fudge sauce

1½ cups homemade or purchased chocolate sauce

1½ cups homemade or purchased butterscotch or caramel sauce

2 jars (7 ounces each) marshmallow cream

4 to 6 tablespoons half-and-half

1 cup coarsely chopped walnuts

1 cup Spanish peanuts

1 cup coarsely chopped toasted almonds

2 pints strawberries, hulled, sliced, and sweetened

Assorted jars of decorative candy sprinkles

8 bananas, peeled and sliced lengthwise

1 jar (10 ounces) maraschino cherries, drained

shake-rattle-and-roll ice cream

2 cups half-and-half

½ cup sugar

3 egg yolks

1 teaspoon vanilla extract

20 cups crushed ice,
  about 7½ pounds

¾ to 1½ cups salt or rock salt

For this family favorite you will need a one-pound can (like a coffee can) with a plastic lid and a three-pound can with a plastic lid.

Makes about 5 cups

In a heavy saucepan over medium heat, bring the half-and-half just to the boiling point. Remove from the heat and cover.

In a bowl, whisk together the sugar and egg yolks until thickened. Stir in the vanilla. Slowly drizzle in the hot half-and-half, whisking constantly. Return to the saucepan and cook over low heat, stirring constantly, until thick enough to coat the back of a spoon. Do not boil. Remove from the heat and cool to room temperature. Pour through a sieve into a clean bowl, cover, and refrigerate for 3 hours.

Pour the chilled custard into a 1-pound can with a plastic lid, cover, and place it in the center of a 3-pound can with a plastic lid. Layer one-fourth of the crushed ice alternately with one-fourth of the salt in the empty space between the two cans. Repeat to create four layers: two layers of crushed ice and 2 layers of salt. Cover the larger can. If the lid isn't secure, reinforce with duct tape.

On a level surface, like a sidewalk, roll the can back and forth for 10 minutes. Pick up the can and shake for 1 minute. Repeat the rolling and shaking for 10 more minutes. The object is to keep the mixture moving.

Open the larger can and pour out the ice and salt. Open the small can and scrape down the sides with a spatula. Stir to re-blend the ice cream. Re-cover the small can. Pack with the remaining ice and salt and secure the lid. Cover, roll, and shake for 5 to 10 more minutes. Check to see if the ice cream is frozen to the desired consistency. If not, replace the lids and shake for 5 more minutes.

blueberry nests

The are no rules for neatness with these crispy treats. Little fingers can press the dough into the muffin tins to make yummy nests for holding a handful of fresh berries. Surprisingly sturdy, the nests make great picnic fare.

1 cup crisp puffed rice cereal, lightly crushed

1/3 cup shredded coconut

1/4 cup finely chopped nuts (optional)

1 cup white chocolate chips, melted and cooled (see note)

1 to 2 cups blueberries

Serves 6

Lightly grease a muffin tin with cooking spray and set aside.

In a bowl, mix together the cereal, coconut, and nuts, if using, until blended. Pour the melted chocolate into the cereal mixture and mix until well combined. With clean, buttered fingers, press 1/3 cup of the cereal mixture into each muffin cup, pressing firmly onto the bottom and sides to form a shell. Place the muffin tin in the refrigerator to chill the shells for at least 20 minutes.

To remove shells, use a knife tip to loosen each nest from its cup. (The nests can be stored in an airtight container at room temperature for up to 5 days.)

Divide the blueberries among the nests, and eat like a cookie or finger tart.

Note: I've found the easiest way to melt white chocolate chips is in the microwave. Curiously, chips often retain their original shape, so you can't tell by peering through the window when they're melted. After 30 seconds on high, open the door and give them a stir. If necessary, repeat in 10-second intervals.

five-spice peach blueberry crisp

Enjoy the fresh fruits of summer, tossed with sugar, and baked in a crisp. What makes this crisp different from others you've tasted is the Chinese five-spice powder in the crumbly topping. A medley of cinnamon, cloves, fennel, star anise, and Szechuan peppercorns, the spice mixture imparts a tantalizing flavor that makes you want to take "just one more bite."

Let the kids lightly grease the baking dish with the butter wrapper. They can also have fun working the chilled butter into the dry ingredients to make the crumbly topping.

Serves 8

Preheat an oven to 350°F. Lightly butter a 10-inch round flameproof baking dish with 2-inch sides (8-cup volume).

Bring a saucepan filled with water to a boil. Add the peaches, one at a time or in batches, and blanch for 15 seconds. With a slotted spoon, transfer the peaches to a colander and rinse under cold water. Using a paring knife, peel, halve, and pit the peaches. Cut each peach into 16 slices, and place the slices in a large bowl. Sprinkle the sugar, cornstarch, and lemon and orange zests over the peaches. Add the blueberries. Toss gently to coat.

In a bowl, stir together the flour, oats, salt, five-spice powder, and brown sugar. Add the butter and, using clean fingers or a pastry blender, work it in until the mixture is crumbly.

Spread the peach and blueberry mixture in the prepared dish. Sprinkle the flour mixture over the peaches. Bake until the juices bubble and the top is browned, about 35 minutes. Serve warm with the vanilla bean ice cream.

6 to 8 ripe peaches (about 2 pounds)

3 tablespoons sugar

3 teaspoons cornstarch

1 teaspoon grated lemon zest

1 teaspoon grated orange zest

1 pint blueberries

2/3 cup all-purpose flour

1/2 cup old-fashioned rolled oats

1/4 teaspoon salt

1/2 teaspoon Chinese five-spice powder

3/4 cup firmly packed light or dark brown sugar

1/2 cup (1 stick) chilled unsalted butter, cut into small pieces

1 quart homemade or purchased vanilla bean ice cream

chocolate p-nut butter candies

Here's no-bake peanut butter candy that's just right for the chocolate lovers in your family. For an extra chocolate surprise, roll the candy dough around an M&M or a chocolate chip.

1/4 cup creamy-style or chunky-style peanut butter

2/3 cup graham cracker crumbs (see note)

1/4 cup chocolate syrup

1/3 cup finely chopped or pulverized peanuts

Makes 1½ to 2 dozen candies

In a bowl, combine the peanut butter, graham cracker crumbs, and chocolate syrup. Stir until well blended. Taste and modify the sweetness or texture by adding more syrup or more cracker crumbs.

Lightly grease the palms of your hands with butter. Take a large marble-sized piece of the dough and roll it into a ball between your palms. Set aside on a platter and repeat until all the dough is used.

Sprinkle the peanuts on a small plate, and roll each ball in the nuts to coat. The candies can be eaten right away or stored in an airtight container in the refrigerator for up to 5 days.

Note: If you don't have graham cracker crumbs, place 12 graham crackers in a plastic bag and crush them by running a rolling pin over the bag several times. Alternately, process the crackers in a food processor or with a handheld blender.

double-chocolate p-nut butter candies

Stir in 2 tablespoons mini chocolate chips before forming the balls. Coat only one-half of each candy with the minced peanuts. Chill the balls for 30 minutes, and then dip the uncoated half in melted chocolate. After dipping, rest the balls on a wire rack to let the chocolate set. Store in an airtight container in the refrigerator for up to 5 days.

index

food

beverages

arctic treat ice cubes, 46
banana smoothie, 41
bianca's extra-lemony sidewalk lemonade, 37
coffee ice cubes, 47
firefly martini, 45
ice cube, 46
kaleidoscope kubes, 47
lime fizz, 39
lime syrup, 39
mocha madness, 42
piña colada shake, 44
pink flamingo punch, 45
p-nut butter banana smoothie, 41
sugar syrup, 37
sunshine tea, 36
sweet lemon zest ice cubes, 47
sweet strawberry lassi, 44
tropical cooler, 40

cookies and candies

chocolate p-nut butter candies, 95
chocolate spanish peanut cookies, 84
double-chocolate p-nut butter candies, 95
fresh fruit cookie pie, 87
silver s'mores, 85
star-spangled cookie, 87
yummy ice cream sandwiches, 84

desserts

blueberry nests, 91
blue-ribbon berry parfaits, 86
five-spice peach blueberry crisp, 93
fresh strawberry shortcake with summer cream, 75
melon-lemon sorbet compote, 64
neighborhood ice cream sundae, 89
shake-rattle-and-roll ice cream, 90

entrées

grilled flank steak, 68
mixed summer grill, 70
super sub sandwich, 62
sweet mama's morning cakes, 67

salads and sides

black bean and corn salsa salad, 53
chile lime butter, 72
clare's potato salad, 73
dad's favorite deviled eggs, 50
deviled caviar eggs, 51
deviled eggs ranchero, 50
gazpacho-to-go, 59
grilled corn-on-the-cob with flavored butters, 71
iceberg wedges with blue cheese dressing, 55
orange mint tabbouleh, 57
roasted garlic butter, 72
roasted greek potato salad, 54
tarragon butter, 71
toasted pecan honey butter, 67
tomato, mozzarella, and basil salad, 56

crafts and decorations

#1 dad gift tags and coupons, 28
ants-in-the-grass citronella candle, 25
big bug bucket, 27
checkerboard star picnic tablecloth, 80
cookie-cutter soaps, 29
fast and fun picture frames, 22
how-your-garden-grows plant markers, 15
keepsake bookmarks, 15
let's-play-jacks frame, 22
mother's heart's delight, 28
one-for-the-road lunch box, 16
pixie sand castles, 14
quick and simple centerpieces, 64
red, white, and blue parade wand, 81
sponge-painted patio pots, 19
stars and stripes dinnerware, 77
sweet hearts and flowers, 30
tiny terra-cotta lamps, 20
vacation place mat, 33
"you're the star" soap-on-a-rope, 30